SCREWING WITH THE SCROOGE

SHAW HART

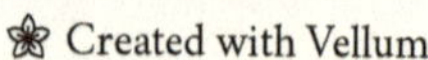 Created with Vellum

It's about to be a very Merry Christmas...

Olive:

Moving to Wolf Valley has been the best decision of my life.

It's the perfect place to run my bakery and it's also where I meet Xavier Grady, the man of my dreams.

He's tall, grumpy, and guarded, my opposite in almost every way, but none of that matters to me. I know that he has secrets and that he's wounded from his time in the military, but that only makes me want to break down his walls even more.

Xavier:

I was finally starting to get used to being back in this small town.

Then Olive Baker moves in across the street from me and flips my life upside down.

I thought I liked my boring life and sleepy town, but now, I'm not so sure.

There's something addictive about the curvy little spitfire that I can't seem to resist.

I know that nothing could happen between us because she could never want a grumpy scrooge like me, but that doesn't stop me from wanting her.

When I finally confess how I feel about her, will it end up being too late, or am I about to get everything that I ever wanted this Christmas?

avier

"SHE'S SCREWING WITH ME," I grumble as I slide into the booth across from my best friend, Townes.

"Who? Olive?" He asks easily as he takes a swig of his coffee.

"Who else do you know in this town that would mess with me?" I spit at him and I see him trying to hide his grin. "It's not funny!" I snap, and he schools his features.

"Of course not," he says condescendingly, and I wonder why I bother to tell him anything. "What did she do now?"

"Decorated," I grit out through my clenched teeth.

My dentist is going to be so upset when he sees how much I've been grinding them lately.

"The horror," Townes deadpans. and I glare at him as I pull out my phone and swipe to the picture that I took this morning.

"Decorated like this," I tell him, showing him the screen.

"With reindeer? Well, it is almost Christmas so... wait," he says, leaning across the table as I zoom in on two of the plastic reindeer that I found in my front yard this morning. "Is that big one mounting Rudolph?"

"Yep," I snarl, dropping my phone onto the table.

Townes is visibly shaking with laughter, and I fight the urge to punch him.

"Coffee?" Ruby asks, already filling up a cup before I can respond.

"Thanks. I'll take the lumberjack breakfast too," I order, and she shakes her head.

"No can do. I have a gift for you instead."

I frown as she ducks behind the counter and comes back with a bakery box. I recognize it instantly and my stomach clenches.

"Olive dropped this off for you this morning. Made fresh. She made me promise that I wouldn't bring you anything else to eat," she says.

"What do you think your boss will say about that?" I ask Ruby.

"I'm fine with it!" Ford, the owner of the diner, calls as he heads over to the register.

Ruby grins at me as she turns and heads to fill up another customer's coffee cup. I glare at the box, and Townes sighs.

"Aren't you going to dig in?" He asks, and I shake my head.

"Nope."

"Can I then?" He asks. "Their pies are my favorite. I hope it's their busting cherries one."

My eyes snap to his and I blink.

"It's not seriously named that," I protest, my mouth dropping open, and Townes laughs.

"I'm sure that it's something like that," he says, and I know that he's right.

Olive moved to town four months ago with her sisters,

and in that short amount of time, they've managed to turn my sleepy, boring town into something that I don't recognize. I used to have a routine. I used to be almost bored. Now, every day it's something new.

I'd never tell her or anyone, but I secretly love that.

The Baker sisters came to Wolf Valley and promptly opened up a bakery, a romance book store, and a sex shop all right next door to each other on Main Street. When I first saw the sign for Masterbeaters, I assumed that there was a misspelling or that the font just made it look weird. I had assumed that they meant to call it MasterBakers.

Then I met the Baker sisters, and I'm positive that isn't the case.

All of them seem to love sexual innuendos and making dirty jokes. They're open and free in a way that is impossible not to be drawn to, no matter how hard I try, and trust me, I try.

She makes it hard though. Not only is she taking over my town, but she also just so happens to be my new next-door neighbor. She moved in across the street from me and has been trying to drive me crazy ever since.

At first, it was just her leaving baked goods on my front porch, but that quickly changed to romance books with half-naked men on the cover. I thought that was bad, but then the sex toys started to arrive.

Since Christmas is right around the corner, I'm guessing that she's decided to move on to leaving inappropriate decorations in my front yard.

"What's her end game?" I mumble to myself, and Townes snorts.

"Uh, you," he says, but I ignore him.

That can't be true. We're polar opposites. No way a spunky ray of sunshine like that goes for a brooding grump like me.

"Why don't you just ask her out already?" Townes asks as he takes a bite of his breakfast.

I stare at his bacon longingly, and he scoots his plate away from me. I glare at him, and he laughs.

"I can't have Ford or Ruby refusing to take my order too, man. One of us should be able to eat," he tells me, and I roll my eyes.

"I'm not asking her out," I say.

"Why not? She's pretty."

My stomach cramps and I try to ignore the jealousy and anger that comes with Townes' words. I don't stop to analyze why I feel that way about Townes noticing Olive.

He's right anyway. Olive is pretty. She's gorgeous, actually. She reminds me of one of the woodland faeries that my mom used to tell me lived in the forests around our house when I was a kid. With her red hair and bright blue eyes, she looks angelic. She's tiny enough to be a fairy too, at only five and a half feet tall.

"Someone else will then," Townes tells me.

"Who?" I blurt out.

I clear my throat, trying to school my features, but we both know that he sees through me.

"Literally anyone with eyes," he informs me, and I glare at him.

"She'll say no."

"How can you be so sure?" He asks me.

"She's a hellion. She won't settle for anyone."

"You think that you're the only one she'll settle for?" He asks me, and I grab my pie.

"She's not into me. She just likes screwing with me," I tell him as I stand. "Now, since I wasn't allowed to order anything," I say, raising my voice as Ruby walks by. She grins at me, and I grumble as I turn back to Townes, "And since you've upset me, you're paying for my coffee."

Townes laughs as I head for the door and scowl as I cross the parking lot and climb into my truck. I set the pie on the passenger seat and sigh. My stomach growls, but I don't dare take a bite of the baked goods. Not when I'm so close to MasterBeaters. With my luck, Olive would pop up and see me devouring it. God knows what she'd do then.

I start the truck, and my heart lodges in my throat when I see a familiar flash of red hair heading down the street. I relax when I see that it's not Olive but her sister, Maple, heading towards their row of shops.

I pull out of the parking lot and head towards home. Traffic is light, like always. Wolf Valley is a small town, nestled between the mountains in Oregon. Like most people who live here, I was born and raised here. I left as soon as I turned eighteen and joined the Army.

That was where I met Townes. We went through boot camp together and then through Army Ranger school after that. When I was shot, we both decided not to re-enlist and instead got out and moved here.

I pass along the road that leads to my childhood home and tense as I see the dark windows of the house that I grew up in. Even from the outside, it looks like a nightmare.

I hit the gas, hurrying past, and a few miles later, I'm pulling onto my street. I can't help it; even though I know that she's probably at the bakery, my eyes still go across the street to Olive's house.

Longing fills me and I hate it.

I hate that I want her more than anything. I shouldn't; I know that any relationship that I have will just end in a disaster.

"You'll never be worth anything. You're nothing but a murderer."

My father's voice fills my head, and I blink, pulling myself out of the bad memories. I grab the pie, my appetite long gone as I head inside.

My house is quiet, and I sigh as I look around, wondering what I should do today. My hip starts to ache, and I know that it's going to storm at some point today.

My phone buzzes, and I wander into the living room as I pull it out and glance at the screen. It's an unknown number, but as soon as I read the message, I know instantly who it is.

UNKNOWN: How did you like my cherry?
Xavier: How did you get my number?

I SAVE her number into my phone.

OLIVE: Townes gave it to me.
Olive: Isn't this great? Now we can talk all the time.
Xavier: Great.
Olive: How was the pie?
Xavier: Haven't tried it yet. Was really looking forward to some pancakes and bacon.
Olive: I can make that for you. Invite me over.

I SHOVE my phone back into my pocket. My emotions are all over the place. I know that she's just messing with me. She's probably like this with everyone. It makes sense since she's so confident and sassy. Everyone in town already loves her.

Still, I can't help but wish that she meant it. I can't help but wish that I could really invite her over and not ruin everything.

I sigh as I head back into the kitchen and eye the pie box.

With a curse, I grab a fork and take a bite. The sugar and tart cherries melt in my mouth, and I grumble as I take another bite.

I try to ignore the image of me eating a different cherry, but I fail. My eyes look out the window towards Olive's house, and I swallow my bite and push the pie box and any thoughts of my curvy little neighbor aside as I get to work.

live

"I'M NOT sure that I'm very good at this flirting stuff," I tell my sisters as I walk into the bakery.

"He didn't like the reindeers?" Saffron asks

"Or the cherry popping pie?" Ginger, my sister, asks as she wipes down the counter in the back of the bakery.

"I'm not sure. He said that he hadn't tried it yet. He didn't mention the reindeer."

"Maybe he didn't see them?" Maple says, and I frown.

"They would be pretty hard to miss."

"Maybe he didn't know that it was you?" Ginger suggests, and I snort.

"No one else really interacts with him. He has to know that it was me."

I sigh as I lean against the counter.

"I thought that he would get the hint by now and ask me out, but I guess not. Maybe he's not interested in me."

"How could he not be! You're amazing!" Saffron says as she sneaks some baked goods out of the case.

"You have to say that because you're my sister and you love me."

"Still," she insists, and I smile.

Maple and Ginger are nodding in agreement, and I try to smile.

"I know. I don't know how he can miss how awesome I am. I'll just have to try harder," I say, but deep down I know that probably isn't the answer.

My sisters go back to cleaning and helping me shut down the bakery. It's getting late and the baked goods are all set for tomorrow so all we need to do is wipe down everything and then we can close up. The bookstore next door is already closed and Wet and Wild, the adult toy store on the other side is being run by Mira, our part-time employee.

I glance at the wall where the bookstore is located. As an avid romance reader, I've thought a lot about what my love story would look like. I liked to imagine that I would bump into my dream man and he would instantly be smitten with me. He would be charming and easy to talk to, and he'd fall head over heels in love with me on the spot and beg to have my phone number to know everything about me. It would be a quick courtship, and then we'd be well on our way to our happily ever after.

Instead, the opposite is happening.

I can still remember the first time that I saw Xavier. He was in town, at the grocery store, and my eyes had been drawn to him. Everyone around him seemed to be avoiding him, giving him a wide berth and looking anywhere but in his direction. He had seemed used to it, his face a stoic mask, but I had seen it.

He was lonely, maybe even a little sad.

I recognized the look well. I had seen it on my face every

day for months after my parents died. Luckily for me, I had my sisters to lean on and pull me out of my funk. Xavier didn't really seem to have anyone.

I had vowed then and there to get to know him and try to make him smile, but it's been four months now and I have yet to succeed.

I've tried everything I could think of. I brought him brownies when I realized that he lived across the street from me. He had been polite but distant then, and the only thing I learned was his name and that he had been born and raised here in town.

The next time I saw him was at the diner in town. I had slid in across from him and told him about my sisters and the shops that we were opening up. I had invited him to the bakery's grand opening, and my heart had soared when I saw him walk in. He never talked to me that day though. He had just scowled at the display case and then slipped out. He seemed uncomfortable to be around so many people and I wondered if he was claustrophobic.

I didn't let him ignoring me that day stop me though. I've spent the last four months learning everything that I could about my grumpy giant. I know that he was in the military and that he was injured, though no one really talks about how or where. Sometimes I've seen him limping on his right side, so I'm guessing it was in his leg or hip. I know that his best friend is Townes, an equally grumpy, though not as brooding man. I know that he hates walnuts, loves being outdoors, and apparently, he has no sense of humor.

I don't know when my attempts at getting to know him turned into me trying to tease or flirt with him. I liked seeing him react whenever I brought him one of my dirty pastries or said some kind of innuendo to him. Those seemed to be the only times that I saw a hint of life behind that mask that he wears so damn well.

Somewhere along the way, I fell in love with him. Maybe I did that first day when I saw him at the market and just didn't recognize the emotion.

I sigh as I close the display case and stretch out my back, rolling my shoulders as I make my way to the office to grab my things.

"Want to come over to my house for dinner?" Saffron asks as we leave.

Ginger and Maple head over to Wet and Wild to relieve Mira, and I smile, waving as they disappear inside.

"No, I'm tired. I'm going to go home and take a bath. Maybe read for a bit before bed. Raincheck?" I ask, and she nods.

"Of course. I'll see you tomorrow."

She squeezes my shoulder as we both head in opposite directions to our cars. Wolf Valley might seem like a strange place for us to settle and try to start businesses, but it's working out. We had first come to this place when we were kids. I think that I was twelve or thirteen, and we were meeting our grandparents for a family camping trip. I had fallen in love with the town and even after we left, I remembered it as this magical place.

None of us wanted to stay in Seattle after our parents died. We wanted a fresh start, and when I suggested Wolf Valley, everyone had agreed. Business has started out a little slow, but it's been picking up ever since Maple and Saffron started marketing. They're both wizards with social media, and I don't know what they're doing, but it's working. Every day I seem to have more orders for my baked goods, and I know that Shelf Indulgence and Wet and Wild have both been doing better too.

We all help each other, but really each business is one of ours. Mine is the bakery, Maple runs the adult toy store, and Saffron the bookstore. Ginger still hasn't decided what she wants to do, but she seems to enjoy handling the marketing and bouncing between places.

I pass by Maple's apartment and turn down the backroad that leads to my little cottage. My sisters all live closer to town, but I wanted something more remote. I fell in love with my house the second that I saw it. It reminds me of what a fairy's house would look like with an overgrown garden and cute curved roof.

The street is dark as I drive down it and I sigh when I glance at Xavier's house and see that all the lights are off.

"It's only eight thirty," I grumble as I park.

Maybe he's out.

He could have left to meet Townes, but I doubt it. I head inside, almost tripping over the strings of Christmas lights that I still need to hang up.

A thought hits me and I grin as I peek across the street at Xavier's dark house.

Should I? Maybe it's time that I stop bothering him. Maybe I should let this crush go. It's clearly not helping things.

Still… an image of Xavier's stoic face shifting, his eyes getting that light in them, like he's secretly happy about my attention floats behind my eyes, and I grin as I grab the first string of lights and tiptoe back outside.

Just one more time, I promise myself.

CHAPTER 3

avier

"No reindeer orgy today?" Townes asks as he climbs out of his Jeep in front of my house.

I scowl at him as I continue to tug the strings of Christmas lights off of my front yard.

"Nope."

"What'd she do today?" He asks, coming to a stop next to me.

"She wrote XOXO all over my yard."

"Aw," he coos, and I glare at him.

"It's just another joke."

"Obviously. That's how everyone would take it. Definitely not her flirting with you and basically writing you a love note out of Christmas lights," he says sarcastically.

I ignore him and the clenching of my gut as I wrap the lights in another tight loop.

I want to believe him. I want Townes to be right, but I know that he's not.

You're not worth my time or attention, my father's angry voice rings out in my head, and I wince, forcing the memories back. My own father couldn't love me. How could anyone else?

Townes sighs, pulling me from my thoughts, and I look over to see him wrapping up another strand.

"She really commits to things, huh?" He asks as he looks at the two other stings that I had already wrapped up.

I glance over, too, and something close to pride squeezes my heart. I try to ignore the feeling as I continue to wrap up the next string of lights.

"That she does."

"Hmm," he says, and I grit my teeth.

I know that he's baiting me, that I shouldn't ask, but my curiosity gets the better of me.

"What?" I snap, and he grins.

"Well, maybe you should mess with her back," he suggests, and I snort.

"Encourage her, you mean?"

"You'd rather she stopped?" He asks quietly, and my stomach drops.

The truth is, no, I don't want her to stop. I love Olive's pranks. I love knowing that she was thinking of me, probably because I'm always thinking of her, and it's nice to know that I'm not alone in my infatuation.

"Just admit that you like her, man. At least to yourself," Townes says, and I frown.

"She wouldn't want me," I say, the words feeling like a punch to my stomach.

"She *does* want you. She's not doing this to anyone else in town. Besides, I've seen you two together. It's nauseating. All these longing looks when the other isn't watching. Both of you blushing."

He pretends to throw up, and I roll my eyes. Hope starts

to grow in my chest and I try to tamp it down. I know how dangerous hope can be.

"It would never work out. I'm better off by myself," I tell him as I finish with my strand and start to gather all of the lights.

Townes sighs, following me across the road to Olive's house. I stack the lights outside of her door, and when I turn around, he's standing there, staring at me, a mixture of concern and pity in his eyes.

"I know about your dad and mom, X. He's wrong. You have to know that. You didn't kill your mom. You were a kid, and she was taking care of you like a good parent would."

I swallow hard, trying not to show how deeply his words hit me. I can feel the color draining from my face, and I grit my teeth.

I hate thinking about my mom's death or anything having to do with my dad, and Townes knows that. I told Townes about the night that my mom was killed one night when we were both drunk after we graduated Ranger school. We both woke up the next day and seemed to have agreed that neither of us would ever mention it again. If he's bringing it up now, it's for a reason.

"And I know that you blame yourself for the accident when we were deployed, but that wasn't your fault either. No one blames you. No one except yourself."

The familiar taste of regret fills my mouth, and I try to take a deep breath, hoping that the cold air will chase it away, but it only seems to amplify it. As soon as he mentioned the accident, it's like I'm back over there. I can almost feel the sand blowing against my face. When I breathe, I can feel the oppressive heat, the sweat trickling down my back. I can hear the screams and yells from my friends.

Townes was the only one who walked away from our last mission unscathed. Well, that's not the right word. I know that what happened affected him too. He was just the only one able to walk away without help.

"I'm not dating her," I whisper, and then I clear my throat, speaking louder. "It wouldn't work."

Townes sighs, seemingly disappointed and I hate him and myself a little bit in that moment. He knows me; he should know that I'm not capable of what he's telling me to do.

"You should try it," he says, and I open my mouth to argue when he interrupts. "Messing with her back."

My mouth snaps shut and we head back to my house in silence, just our boots crunching on the snow filling the stillness around us.

I'm not sure that what he's suggesting is a good idea, but I can't deny that the thought of getting Olive back, at being closer to her, even in this small way, has my heart racing.

"I'm not good at pranks."

"Can't be that hard," Townes says with a shrug. "Make her a dessert with salt or fill her front yard with gnomes doing it. Hell, Google it. I'm sure that you'd be able to come up with a few ideas."

I smile at his words and grin when I get an idea.

"Alright."

His eyebrows shoot up, disappearing under his wool hat.

"Really?" He asks, and I nod.

"Yeah, I'll try it."

He smiles, clapping me on the back, and I roll my eyes.

"Now, are you going to help me shovel my driveway?" I ask him, and he starts backing up.

"You know, I think that I have somewhere to be," he starts, and I laugh, tossing him a shovel.

He catches it easily, and we fall into a comfortable silence as we start to work on shoveling away the snow that had fallen last night.

"What about you?" I ask him once we're done."

"I already did my driveway."

"No, idiot. When are you going to find a nice girl and settle down?"

"Is that what you're doing?"

"No," I rush to say, but he gives me a knowing smirk. "Shut up," I grumble.

He smiles, leaning on his shovel, and I eye him.

"Is there someone in town?" I ask him, and he blinks.

That's a yes.

"Nope," he lies, and I stare at him.

"Townes."

"No, let's get your love life figured out before we try to add any more. I have a feeling that you're going to need both of our undivided attention to make it through this," he teases, and I flip him off.

"I'm not that hopeless," I tell him, and he doesn't answer, but I know that we're both thinking it.

Yes, I am.

"What's your plan?" He asks, and I take his shovel, hanging them both up in the garage.

"Are you going to help?" I ask him, and he nods.

"Of course."

"Got any carrots?" I ask, and he blinks and then starts to grin.

"Nope, come on though. I'll drive us to the market."

We hop in his Jeep and I smile to myself as we head into town. Nerves are filling me as we head into the store and over to the produce section. I'm not sure how many to buy, so I grab three big bags of carrots and head to checkout.

Townes seems more confident with this plan than I feel, and I try to relax as we head back to my place.

"How many are we making?" He asks as we stare at Olive's front yard.

"Five? Six?" I say, and he nods.

We head to opposite ends of the yard and both start to roll snow. Hours later, when we're done and admiring our work, I can't help but laugh.

"I think that she'll like it," Townes says before he takes the water bottle from me and chugs the whole thing down. "She better anyway," he mumbles, and I grin.

We're both exhausted and sore from working for the last few hours, but as I study Olive's yard, I have to agree. I think that she's going to love it.

"When will she be home?" He asks, and I glance at my phone.

"Shit, soon."

"I kind of want to stay and see her reaction, but I'm sure that you'll tell me about it later. I need a shower, and so do you."

He tosses me the empty water bottle and I catch it, waving at him as he heads back to his Jeep. He waves once before he turns and heads off down the road.

I hurry inside, taking a quick shower. I want to be outside when Olive gets home so that I can see her reaction.

I grab a shovel, pretending to scrape away some more snow from my driveway as I hear Olive's car turn onto our street. I smile, my heart racing in my chest as I see her slow in front of our houses.

When I look up, she's watching me and she smiles at me brightly, waving before she starts to turn into her driveway. That's when she slams on the brakes, and I huff out a laugh when I see her mouth drop open and her eyes go wide.

There, on her front lawn, are six different snowman couples, all in various sexual poses. Her cheeks turn a bright shade of pink as she stares at the one where the male snowman has bent over his partner, and I feel my cock start to harden as I imagine Olive and me in that same position.

She pulls into her drive and hurries to climb out. She looks from the snowman to me and her whole face lights up.

I know then that I'm in trouble, but as she smiles at me, I can't seem to bring myself to care or to brace for the inevitable crash.

CHAPTER 4

Olive

"For me?" I ask Xavier as I cross the road to where he's standing.

"Figured it was time to get you back," he says in his gruff voice.

"I love it," I tell him as I beam up at him, and he swallows.

"Good, because it took hours," he grumbles, and I grin.

"I knew that you had it in you," I say, and he shakes his head.

"I was just trying to give you a taste of your own medicine."

I freeze, doubt curdling inside of me, but when I glance at Xavier, I can see that he doesn't really mean that. There's a light in his eyes like he's happy to have made me so happy, like maybe he even had fun pranking me back.

He looks almost… vulnerable as he watches me now. Like

the rules between us have changed and he's not sure how to proceed.

"You know what?" I ask him as I take a seat on his front porch.

"What?" He asks, sitting down next to me.

"I think that deep down, you would be sad if I ever stopped messing with you."

"You could try it and we could see," he suggests, but there's no force behind his words.

"Did you like the lights this morning?" I ask him, and he huffs out what I'm going to take as a laugh.

"Took me a second to read them."

"Yeah, it was a lot harder to write with Christmas lights than I thought it would be."

The wind picks up and I shiver.

"Invite me in for some hot chocolate," I tell him, and he glances back at his house.

"I don't have any hot chocolate."

"Of course you don't," I sigh, and he frowns.

"Not everyone has hot chocolate," he points out like him not isn't some fatal flaw.

"Sure, sure," I say, patting his knee and he tenses. "Have you eaten yet?"

He blinks at that subject change and shakes his head.

"Okay, come on."

I push to my feet and start across his yard to my place. I weave my way through the snowman, grinning as I take in each pose.

"Very creative," I say when we get to the pair doing it up against the side of my house.

"Thanks. Townes helped."

I grin, waving him inside, and he hesitates before he enters. He's so tall and big that he takes up all of the room inside my house. I have to push past him just to wiggle out of my coat, and he clears his throat.

"I should go," he starts, and I grab his hand.

"We're eating, remember?"

He doesn't say anything as I lead him into the kitchen, but I notice that when I let his hand go, his fingers flex, like maybe he misses me touching him.

Saffron would have swooned at that move. She's made me watch Pride and Prejudice a dozen times and we always have to rewatch when Mr. Darcy helps Elizabeth into the carriage.

"Is chili okay?" I ask, taking out the Tupperware from the fridge.

"Sure, sounds good."

I grab a pot and heat the chili up, grabbing cheese from the fridge and crackers out of the pantry.

"Have a seat," I tell Xavier as I move to grab two spoons.

He winces as he takes a seat at my little dining table, and I pause.

"Are you okay?" I ask him, and he nods.

"I'm fine."

"Didn't look like it," I comment as I grab the milk and two cups.

"It's my hip. It always gets a little sore in the cold."

"Want some Tylenol?" I offer him as I pass him a glass of milk.

He shakes his head, taking a sip.

"How about a bath? I could join you."

He coughs, nearly spraying milk all over the table, and I grin.

"Is that a yes then?"

He clears his throat, and I smile as I head back to the now hot chili. I grab two bowls and ladle chili into each before I join him back at the table.

"You always surprise me," he says quietly as I set a bowl in front of him.

"Is that a good thing?" I ask, and he stares at me for a beat.

"Yeah," he finally admits, and my heart almost bursts in my chest.

"Good. Now, dig in while it's still hot."

He grabs his spoon, and I study him. He looks more relaxed today. His mask has slipped a bit and I can see that vulnerable side that he rarely lets anyone see. He doesn't look as lonely or sad today either and I smile.

"How did you hurt your hip?" I ask, picking up our conversation from earlier.

"I was shot."

"Shit."

He doesn't look up at me; just nods and I swallow.

"When you were deployed," I guess, and that gets another nod. "Is that why you got out?"

"Yeah. Recovery was a while and I knew that I would never be able to operate at one hundred percent again. I didn't want to let my team down by staying in."

"I'm sure that you wouldn't have let them down," I argue, and he shakes his head.

"Rangers, any military squad, relies on each person. Everyone needs to be on top of their game or people die."

There's something in his words and the tone of his voice that has my appetite vanishing.

"You blame yourself for getting shot," I say.

It's a guess, but I know that I'm right.

"It was my fault."

"I doubt that."

He swallows a bite of chili, and I watch him. I wish that I could take away some of his pain, but I don't know how to. Other than by being myself.

"You met Townes in the military, right?"

"Yeah, in Army boot camp. He was my bunkmate and we just clicked. His dad was military, and he was determined to become a Ranger, so we both went there after basic training."

"He seems like a good guy."

"He is. He's the best."

He's relaxed, and I stick to lighter topics as we finish eating.

"Where was your favorite place?" I ask him as he helps me carry the dishes over to the sink.

"I liked Italy. We weren't there for very long, but the food was good. Germany was cool, too."

"I'd love to go there sometime," I sigh, and he almost smiles.

"I'm sure you will. One day."

I load the dishwasher and he puts the milk back in the fridge.

"I should get going."

"Okay, I'll walk you out."

"Thanks for dinner," Xavier says as he tugs his coat and hat back on.

"Sure thing, and listen," I say, leaning against the door as he makes his way down the front porch steps. He stops and turns back to me. "This was a good first date, but I expect you to plan the next one."

His mouth drops open and he looks shocked as I grin at him and close the door. It takes him a minute, but I hear his footsteps as he makes his way back to his place, and I smile as I turn and get ready for bed.

Suddenly, I can't wait to wake up and see what tomorrow has in store for us.

CHAPTER 5

avier

TOWNES SHOWS up at my house bright and early the next day, two to-go cups of coffee in his hands, and I take mine gratefully, draining half of the cup while he makes himself at home on my couch.

"So? How did the snowmen go over?" He asks, and I swallow.

"Good. She liked them anyway."

"Yeah?" He asks, clearly hinting for me to go on.

"I ate dinner with her last night," I admit, and he grins.

"I should write a book," he jokes. "How to win over a girl that is clearly already in love with you. I could give talks all over."

"She's not in love with me," I argue, and he rolls his eyes.

"She is, but don't worry, she seems to like this whole clueless thing that you have going on."

I flip him off, and he laughs as he lifts his cup of coffee and takes a drink.

"How did your first date go then?" He asks, and I scowl.

"It wasn't a date, it was just…an accident," I finish lamely.

"Yeah? And how does one *accidentally* go out on a date?"

I open my mouth to say… what? That it was just a coincidence? Convenient for the two of us to eat together? None of those are really true.

"It was a date," Townes promises me.

"This was a good first date, but I expect you to plan the next one."

Olive's words from last night hit me as I drain the rest of my coffee. I've been thinking about what she said all night. It's obvious that the ball is in my court now, but I have no idea what to do with it.

"I can't date," I tell him.

"X, you already are. Watching you two dance around each other was cute in the beginning, but you're going to lose her. Don't do that," he warns me.

"She told me that the next date was on me," I admit, and he grins, clapping his hands together once in excitement.

"Good. Ask her out. For real this time," he stresses.

"And then what?"

"Then you go out. You learn more about her, maybe kiss her, maybe—"

I cut him off before he can go on.

"This feels like a bad idea."

"It's not. It's the best idea that you've ever had."

"It's *your* idea," I protest, and he laughs.

"I'm a genius. Now, hurry up and get ready to go. She'll probably be between rushes at the bakery so you can ask her out in peace before you chicken out."

He waves his hands at me until I stand and stomp my way into my bedroom. I brush my teeth and stare at my reflection in the mirror. My dark brown hair is getting long and I shove it back from my forehead. The waves stick up in some spots, but I'll be wearing a hat so I don't bother to try to fix it.

Stubble coats my jaw and I debate shaving, but Townes is right. If I want to catch her and ask her out without an audience, then I need to get to the bakery fast.

I tug on my boots and grab my coat and hat. Townes is already standing by the door and he heads out.

"Do you want me to come with?" He offers, and I shake my head.

"I'll be okay."

He nods, clapping me on the shoulder as he heads over to his Jeep.

"I'm headed over to Foster's place. That storm last night took out a tree so we're going to cut it up as best we can, move it out of the way, and all that. You should come help."

"I will," I promise him, and he waves as he climbs into his car and heads back down the road.

I take a deep breath as I climb into my truck, letting it warm up before I shift into drive and head into town.

I can't believe that I'm doing this, and those feelings are only amplified when I drive by my childhood home.

I grew up hearing about how I killed my mom and how I wasn't worth anything. I was the bane of my father's existence, and leaving to join the Army was supposed to my way of proving him wrong.

My hips aches and I shift in my seat, rubbing the spot where I was shot. I know that I should take it easy today, rest it, but I have a feeling that Townes will hunt me down if I don't go help with Foster's tree.

The bakery comes into view, and I take a deep breath.

It's just a date. Just dinner. I'm just trying to even the score since she cooked for me, I tell myself as I park out front and head inside before I can talk myself out of this.

I feel like I'm going to throw up as I walk in the door. The scent of her baked goods has my mouth watering, and I take a few deep breaths as I walk up to the counter.

"Be right with you!" She calls from the back, and I debate bolting back out to my truck.

Abort! This is not a good idea. When I inevitably mess this all up, then things are going to be really awkward. I'll have to see her all of the time and –

Olive comes out of the back smiling at something on her phone, and my heart kicks so hard against my ribs that I'm surprised none of them break.

Fuck.

I want her.

It's been so long since I've wanted anything. I've learned to just get by with what I have, to not ask for too much, but dammit, I need her. I somehow know that if she ever left me, it would ruin me. I would never be able to survive that loss. Still, the chance of being with her is worth the risk.

"Xavier," she says with a bright smile as her green eyes meet mine.

She looks like a mischievous fairy, and I want to see what kind of trouble we can get into.

"Have dinner with me," I blurt out.

My voice comes out low and gravely, and I see her shiver as her face brightens.

"Sure? Any special occasion?" She asks, teasing me, and I bite back my own smile.

"It's a date."

She nods, looking serious for a beat as she studies me.

"Alright," she agrees quietly.

I stare at her. It feels like something huge just shifted between us. There are no more games or pranks to hide behind. It's not just teasing now. This is real. We've both just admitted that we want this with the other and there's no going back now.

"I'll see you tonight."

"Okay, I'm off at four today."

"I'll come by your place at five to get you then."

She nods, and I want to reach for her. I want to squeeze her hand or wipe the trace of flour from her cheek, but the door opens behind me, and instead, I take one last look at her and then head back out to my truck.

I'm both relieved and anxious as I climb behind the wheel and head over to help my friends.

At least she said yes.

Now I just need to figure out what to do tonight on our date.

CHAPTER 6

live

XAVIER SHOWS up on my doorstep at exactly five o'clock. An excited buzz skates along my skin as I smooth my hair down and go to answer the door.

I had raced home from the bakery and thrown myself into the shower, scrubbing all of the flour, sugar, and frosting off of me. I had a special dress that I bought for myself for my birthday last year. It was way too much money and I'd never had an occasion to wear it, but when Xavier invited me to dinner, I knew that I would be wearing it tonight. The crushed velvet fabric clings to my curves and the dark blue color reminds me of Xavier's eyes.

I pull the door open, love and lust bubbling up inside of me as I take in Xavier's imposing form. He's all bundled up and holding a Norfolk pine tree in his hands.

"Hey," I say after we've stared at each other for a solid minute.

Xavier blinks, tearing his eyes away from my body, and I grin. It seems the dress is a hit with him too.

"Hey," he says, clearing his throat and thrusts the little tree at me. "I got this for you. It seemed like it would last longer than flowers," he explains, and I smile at how practical he is.

"Thanks. It's cute. I'll have to decorate it with some ornaments later."

He nods, shifting on his big feet, and I set the tree on the entryway table and grab my coat.

"Where are we headed?" I ask as I stuff my arms through the sleeves and grab my purse.

"Um, I thought that I would cook for you. If that's okay?"

"Of course!"

I thread my fingers through his arm, partly because I'm going to need help navigating the snowy and icy road in my heels and also because I want an excuse to touch him.

"I can carry you," he says after a beat, and I beam up at him.

"Alright."

No sooner is the word out of my mouth when Xavier has leaned down and swooped me up into his arms. My mouth drops open slightly and I'm stunned into silence, but Xavier seems unfazed as he strides easily across the street and up to his house.

As soon as we're inside, he sets me on my feet and I instantly kick off my shoes and shrug out of my jacket. He takes my coat, disappearing for a moment.

"I like your place," I say as I look around.

It's kind of empty with no personal effects in sight, but it still feels warm. There's a fire roaring in the living room. A giant flat screen hangs on the wall above the fireplace and a pair of comfortable and butter-soft leather couches are on either wall.

"Thanks."

He toes off his own boots and takes off his coat and hat.

"Can I help with dinner?" I ask as I follow him into the kitchen.

"No, I wanted to cook for you."

I smile as he pulls out a stool for me at the counter.

"Want something to drink? I, um, got a bottle of wine... and some hot chocolate,," he mumbles, and I bite back my smile.

"For me?" I ask, and I see his cheeks heat slightly.

"It just sounded good when you said it yesterday," he mumbles, and I snort.

"Uh-huh. Okay, then let's both have some hot chocolate."

I see him try to hide his disgusted look, but he nods, pulling down two mugs and filling them with milk. He puts the cups in the microwave and then grabs the container of hot chocolate mix.

"Oh, you got the good stuff, too," I say as I take in the Ghirardelli label.

He ignores me as he opens the container and grabs two spoons, but I could swear that he looks happy that I approve of his hot chocolate choice.

He moves stiffly around the kitchen like maybe he doesn't spend a lot of time in this room and isn't comfortable. The microwave beeps, and he grabs the cups, topping them off with heaping spoonfuls of the chocolate mix.

"Looks good," I compliment as he passes me a cup.

I take a small sip, meeting his eyes and he sighs as he lifts his own cup to his lips and shudders through a drink.

"Admit it! You hate it," I say with a laugh, and he grimaces.

"It's too sweet," he complains, and I giggle.

"Well, I'm touched that you got it for me. It means a lot that you were thinking of me."

He ducks his head, but I can see the blush spreading

down his neck as he turns to the stove and grabs a few pots.

"Are you sure that I can't do anything?" I ask him as I take another drink of hot chocolate.

"No, I've got it."

I watch as he fills up a pot with water and unscrews a jar of spaghetti sauce, dumping it into the other pan.

"How was your day?" I ask him.

"Good. I went over to a friend's house and helped them cut up a tree that fell down."

"With your shirt off?" I ask, making my voice breathy, and he shakes his head.

"No, it was below freezing so we all stayed fully clothed," he says, sounding amused at my dirty mind.

"Pity. Is it okay if in my head, you were all shirtless?" I ask, and then Xavier does something that shocks me.

His head tilts back and he laughs. The sound is deep and rusty, washing over me like a wave, and I stare at him in shock. His deep blue eyes are crinkled and shining so brightly as he stares at me across the kitchen island. His teeth flash, stark white against his dark stubble.

This is it. My first Xavier smile, and man, it does not disappoint. This man was made to smile. To grin, and smirk, and laugh.

"You always surprise me," he says, his smile fading, and I blink.

"Is that still a good thing?"

"Yes," he says simply, and my body warms.

"What did you do?" He asks as he adds the pasta to the boiling water.

"I had an order for a penis cake and some cupcakes," I tell him, and he nods like it's normal. "It's for Cindy's bachelorette party."

"Ah, I just figured that it was another Thursday for you," he says, and I laugh.

"Nope, this one was special."

"Who is running the bakery right now?" He asks as he stirs the pasta.

"It's closed now, but Ginger shut down for me today."

"She's the youngest of your sisters, right?" He asks, and I nod.

"Yeah, it goes me, Maple, Saffron, and then Ginger."

"All food names," he comments, leaning back against the stove to study me.

"Yeah, my mom was obsessed with cooking. She had gone to culinary school, but then she met my dad and got pregnant with me so she never really worked in a kitchen."

"She didn't want to?"

"No, chef hours are crazy long. She always said that she was happy to just cook for us. She was good at it too," I say with a wistful smile.

"I'm sorry," he says softly, picking up on my somber tone, and I nod.

"She had cancer. Passed when I was sixteen."

"Olive," he says, and I clear my throat.

"My dad wasted away after that. She was the love of his life. I wasn't even that surprised when he passed away from a heart attack when I was eighteen."

We're silent, and he watches me.

"Shit, sorry, I didn't mean to make things so heavy on our date."

"No, it's okay. My… my mom passed away when I was a kid too," he admits, and I can see the pain those words still bring him.

"I'm so sorry, Xavier."

He nods, staring at his feet as he swallows hard.

"I was sick and she went out to get me my medicine. It was storming, practically a blizzard. She went off the road and hit a tree," he says, and my heart breaks for him.

I reach over the island, grab his hand and he startles from his memories. He looks up, his dark blue eyes meeting mine and clinging. We stare at each other, pain and a certain understanding passing between us.

We're both at least a little broken, but that doesn't scare me away from him. It makes me like him even more.

Smoke catches my eye and I gasp, dropping his hand and pointing behind him.

"Shit!" He shouts, hurrying to turn off the burners and try to save the food.

I stand, moving to see if I can help, and I bite my lip as I take in the now ruined food.

"I can't really cook," he admits with a sigh, and I blink.

"Were you trying to scare me off by offering to cook for me?" I ask him, and his head whips to me.

"What? No! Wait…did I?" He asks, sounding panicked, and I shake my head.

"No, but you should have told me. I would have been happy to help."

"I wanted you to relax. You make food for people all day," he says, and I melt a little bit.

"I like cooking. I wouldn't have minded."

"I just wanted to take care of you a little bit."

"You did. You saved me from that treacherous road," I point out, taking a step closer to him.

He eyes me warily, and I laugh.

"Should we order something? Or I can run out and grab us something."

"Let's see what you have here."

I pull open the fridge and then peek into his cabinets. He doesn't have much, and I end up grabbing some bread and lunch meat.

"How about a sandwich?" I ask.

"Sounds good."

We work side by side as we assemble our sandwiches. I finish my hot chocolate, and Xavier passes me his cup without a word. I smile as I lift it to my mouth and drink from the same spot that he did.

"Want to watch a movie?" He asks.

"A Christmas one?" I ask, and he shrugs.

"Sure."

We settle onto one of his couches and I take a bite of my sandwich. He passes me the remote and I start to flip through the channels, trying to find a Christmas movie.

"We always watch How The Grinch Stole Christmas every year," I tell him with a smile. "What about you?"

"I don't really have a lot of holiday traditions," he admits.

"Really? What are you doing this year?"

"Just hanging out around here. I'm sure that I'll hang out with Townes, maybe grab dinner at his place or something."

My heart cracks a fraction. That has to be so lonely.

"Come over to my place. We'll all be together. You can bring Townes."

"Maybe. I'll ask Townes," he says, and I smile.

"You'll be there. Stop playing hard to get," I tell him, knocking my knee against his.

He huffs out a laugh, smiling as he bites into his sandwich.

A Christmas Story comes on, and I leave it, setting the remote on the couch beside me. We quickly finish our sandwiches and I smile when I see how stiff he is as he sits next to me.

I'm finally having my first date, watching a movie with a boy, and I'm not about to pass up this opportunity. I have no experience with guys, nothing to go on except for my romance books and rom-com movies. Still, I want this, and I'm not afraid to go after what I want.

"Brr, I'm cold," I say, sidling closer to him on the couch.

"I'll add some more wood to the fire," he says as he takes a drink from his glass of water.

"Or," I start, "we could cuddle. I could even feel you up a little bit," I suggest, and he chokes, spraying water across the coffee table.

I giggle, and his mouth drops open as he turns to face me.

"It's not safe to drink around you," he mumbles, and I full-on laugh then.

"I like keeping you on your toes."

"Feel me up," he says under his breath, huffing out a laugh. "Wait…do you want to?" He asks incredulously, and I laugh.

"Uh yeah. If I could figure out a way to convince you to take off your shirt while I did it, I would totally suggest that too. I've been dreaming about it since I first saw you. I don't want you to think that I'm just after you for your body, though."

He blushes at my words, and I wonder how much experience he has with all of this too. He looks amazed at my words like the thought that anyone could want him is so foreign. For the first time, I wonder just how much, if any, experience Xavier has with dating and women.

There's something in his eyes as he looks at me that reminds me of an abandoned puppy who is too afraid to hope that he'll ever be wanted. The look breaks my heart, and suddenly, I'm so glad that we moved to Wolf Valley and that I met him.

I vow right then and there that I'm going to show him just how amazing he is. I'm already getting him to let down his guard and open up to me, so how hard could it be?

I lean towards him and he looks down to my lips as I close the distance between us.

CHAPTER 7

avier

Holy shit.

Olive's lips are on mine and she's feeling me up. Her hands are running greedily over my body and I can't seem to wrap my mind around it.

Fuck. She wants me just as badly as I want her. How is that even possible?

She moans against my mouth as I kiss her back, my hands cradling her face as she opens beneath me. I don't waste any time in slipping my tongue into her mouth to tangle with hers.

Her fingers dip beneath my shirt, and I shiver as her short nails skim across my skin, leaving goosebumps in their wake.

My cock is hard and pressing against the zipper of my jeans. For a moment, I'm concerned that he might break right through.

Fuck.

I've been hit on before, but I never was interested. I can't even remember any of their faces. There's only Olive. She's all that I see.

I've been dreaming about her for months, but in my dreams, it was always me as the instigator. For a second, I wonder if maybe I've finally lost it. Maybe this is all a dream.

I reach up, pinching myself, and I curse against her mouth at the sting.

"What was that?" she asks breathlessly.

"I pinched myself," I admit.

"Any particular reason?" She asks, laughter dancing in her green eyes.

"I thought that this might be a dream."

Her eyes soften at that and she smiles softly.

"You say the nicest things," she murmurs, and my heart starts to thud loudly in my ears.

"I do?"

"To me anyway," she says, and I nod.

"Only you."

"I like that," she admits, and her lips move closer to mine.

Her red hair is mussed, tangled in a halo around her head, and I swallow hard.

"I've never…" I start, and she blinks.

"Me neither."

"How is that possible?" I blurt, and she laughs.

"No one ever caught my eye."

But I did?

I want to ask her, but my cock is begging me to shut up and explore those curves that we've been picturing for months.

My hands cradle her face and she leans into my touch. Her mouth meets mine and I moan as she slips her tongue into my mouth. She shifts next to me and I reach for her instinctively. She swings a leg over mine and straddles me.

"Olive," I groan, my fingers tightening on her hips as she settles over me.

"I ache," she moans, and I'm spurred into action.

I need to give this girl anything that she needs. It's a necessity to me, like air. I want to be her man. I want to be the only one that she aches for. I want to take it away as many times as she'll let me.

I tug the soft fabric of her dress up to her hips and she wiggles on top of me. I grit my teeth, willing myself not to come as she pulls the zipper down. I tug the dress over her head and my eyes slam closed.

I think about being shot, about being deployed, anything except for Olive's perfect body on top of mine.

When I blink my eyes open, she's watching me, her face flushed. She's wearing black lace and I want to tear it off of her and bury my tongue, fingers, and cock inside of her until she screams.

"Xavier," she begs, and I drag her mouth back to mine as my other hand explores her body.

She arches against me, her fingers fumbling with the buttons on my shirt.

"Rip it," I order her, and she blinks, a hot smirk coming to her lips as she looks up at me.

"Really?"

"Yes."

She tears at either side of the fabric, sending buttons flying.

"I've always wanted to do that," she admits, and I nod.

"You can do it to all of my shirts," I promise her, and she laughs, her mouth smiling as she presses a kiss to my throat.

I want to tell her that I'm not joking, but her hands are on my bare skin, and I reach for her instead.

I unhook her bra, groaning as her tits spill out. They fit

perfectly in my hands, and I run my thumbs over her hard nipples until she's gasping and squirming on top of me.

She frowns down at my jeans and I stand, dumping her onto the couch cushions as I unbutton and push my jeans and boxers down.

"Damn," she breathes, her eyes locked on my dick.

I'm worried that maybe I've moved too fast, that maybe she's about to change her mind. I debate reaching for my boxers at least, but before I can move, Olive has slid off of the couch and is kneeling before me.

"I might be terrible at this," she warns, and I swallow.

"You're already doing amazing."

She smiles, emboldened by my words, and I watch, standing still as a statue as she wraps her fingers around my length.

She looks up at me from under her lashes, and I swear that I almost come from that look alone.

"Perfect," I whisper, and she rewards me with a single pump.

Her creamy skin is on full display, and I'm not sure where to look first. Her tits are swaying gently as she shuffles forward, her mouth even with my cock now.

She licks her lips, and I groan. When she wraps her lips around me, her tongue flicking over the tip of my dick, I bite down so hard on my cheek that I taste blood.

I'm not going to last, but when I look down at Olive, she looks so happy. I grit my teeth, determined to last a little longer at least.

Her head bobs on my length, and I swallow hard, my breathing turning ragged as I watch her.

"Fuck, Olive," I groan, and she hums around me.

"Shit. I'm going to come. You have to stop," I warn her, and she only sucks harder. "Olive."

My fingers tighten in her hair and she moans at the pressure.

That's what does it; feeling her moans of pleasure around me has my balls tightening up and I groan as I come in her mouth. She swallows around me, and my eyes roll back in my head at the sensation.

"Fuck," I hiss, and she licks her lips.

My cock jerks at the sight, and I pant.

"Lay back on the couch," I order, and she pushes herself back onto the cushions. "Look at you," I say as she stretches out before me. "So damn beautiful."

She reaches a hand out to me, and I walk over to the armrest, grabbing her legs and dragging her towards me.

My mouth waters as I stare down at her spread out before me. I have to taste her. I want to make her scream my name until she's hoarse. I want her to dream about me the same way that I dream about her.

I reach up, pinching one of her nipples, and she gasps, arching up off of the couch. I smile, setting her legs over my shoulders as I kneel at the end of the couch. Her ass is resting on the armrest, and I kiss the inside of her thigh once before I bury my face in her cunt.

"Xavier! Oh!" She screams, and I smile.

I tongue her snug opening, licking a path back up to her clit and circling the little bundle of nerves. I eat at her, listening to her moan and scream and beg me for more.

Her juices are covering my face and dripping down my chin and I love it. I want to bathe in it. I want to walk around smelling like her pleasure for the rest of my life.

Her hands tangle in my hair, her legs locking around my head and I slip the tip of my tongue into her pussy as she goes off.

"Xavier!" She screams, her whole body tensing as she comes all over my face.

I drink down her release, greedy for it. She trembles against me before her body goes lax, and I kiss her clit once more before I stand, licking my lips.

I smile when I look down at her and see she's fast asleep. She looks so sweet, her hair in disarray around her face. Her lips are turned up, even in her sleep, and I huff out a laugh at that as I gather her in my arms and carry her into my bedroom. She curls up onto her side as I tuck her in and go out to add another log to the fire.

I gather up our clothes and carry them into my room, dumping them on the dresser. I slip on a pair of boxers, debating what to do, but I can't resist the chance to sleep next to her.

I climb into bed, and she rolls towards me, cuddling against my side. I smile, wrapping my arms around her as I close my eyes and let sleep claim me, too.

CHAPTER 8

live

I'M SO USED to waking up before the sun, so when I first open my eyes, it's not the strange bedroom that has me confused. It's the fact that the room is sunny.

"Shit!" I shout, jackknifing up in bed.

"Wha?" Xavier croaks, lifting his head up off the pillow as I crawl over his body and start to frantically search for my clothes.

"I'm late! I'm so, so late," I explain as I tug my dress over my head and wiggle it over my curves.

Going to work like this is not ideal, but if I run home and change then I'm going to be even more late.

Xavier sits up in bed, and I stumble as I pull on one shoe, my eyes locked on the wide expanse of his chest. His muscles are on full display, and a secret thrill shoots through me when I remember that I had my hands and mouth on the body just last night.

"I'll drive you. Here, you can borrow some clothes."

He tosses me a shirt, and I wiggle out of my dress and pull the soft material over my head. He passes me a pair of sweatpants and I pull those on next. The outfit looks strange since it's obviously two sizes too big. The high heels also don't help, but beggars can't be choosers.

"Thanks," I say, and he grunts back at me.

He pulls on his shoes, and I head for the front door. I'm about to pull the door open when a hand grabs my elbow and I'm spun around to face a grumpy-looking Xavier.

"What?" I ask, and he grabs his winter jacket.

"It's freezing. You can't go out in just my shirt."

He holds the jacket open for me and I pause.

"I wore my coat last night," I remind him.

"I know, but mine is warmer and since I don't have time to go warm the truck up for you," he says, wiggling the coat at me.

I smile as I turn and stuff my arms in. It's sweet that he's looking out for me, that he wants to take care of me. It's been a while since I had that.

He zips the zipper up to my chin and then nods.

"Let's go."

He takes my hand as we head for the front door, and I smile, letting him lead me over to his truck. He opens my door for me, and I take the time to lean up on my toes and press my mouth to his.

"What was that for?" He asks as he grabs my hips and lifts me into his truck.

I've got to say; I can see why all of the heroines in my romance books love being manhandled by their men.

"Do I need a reason to kiss you?" I ask him, and he smiles softly.

"Nope."

I laugh as he closes the door and rounds the hood. He

cranks the truck up, and I bury my face in his shirt, breathing in his woodsy scent.

"What are you doing today?" I ask him as we head towards town.

It's still early and the roads are mostly deserted.

"I need to clean up the disaster that was dinner last night," he says, and I laugh.

"I'm sure that it would have been great. I just distracted you."

"You've been doing that since you got to town," he admits, and I beam, looking over at him.

He's wearing his own shirt and sweatpants combo, but he fills his out a lot better than I do.

We pull up in front of the bakery a minute later and for the first time since I opened MasterBeaters, I wish that I didn't have to go to work.

"I'll see you later?" I ask, and he nods.

"Yeah."

I wish that we had a date set up, but I know that I need to get inside so I wave and hurry out of the truck. Xavier is halfway around the front of the truck and he sighs as I slam the door closed.

"I'll get your door from now on," he says, and I grin.

"Every door?" I ask with a laugh, and he doesn't answer me.

Instead, he just silently walks over to the bakery door and grips the handle. I pass him the key and he unlocks the door and holds it open for me, dropping my keys in my palm as I pass.

"Thanks," I say, and he nods.

I almost slip in my heels as I hurry behind the counter. Luckily, I prepped a lot of things last night so I shouldn't be too late on opening.

I get to work, washing up and preheating the ovens. I get

the first batch in and start to set up the display case when there's a knock on the door. I frown, looking up and my eyes widen when I see Xavier standing there, a pair of my sneakers dangling from his fingers.

"How did you get those?" I ask him as he pushes past me inside.

"Your spare key is under the mat."

"It is," I confirm, and he passes me the shoes.

"You couldn't work in those all day. I grabbed you this stuff too. Figured that you would be more comfortable in your own clothes."

He passes me a bag, and I smile when I see a pair of jeans and a clean t-shirt.

"So you broke into my house?"

"Yep."

"And they say chivalry is dead."

His cheeks and the tips of his ears turn red and I think that I fall a little more in love with Xavier right then and there.

"Thanks for doing this."

"It's no big deal."

I want to argue with him, to tell him that it is, that it's been a long time since anyone has looked out for me. As the oldest, I'm usually the one making sure that everyone is okay and has what they need.

Instead of telling Xavier any of that, I wrap my arms around his neck and press my lips against his. His hands land on my hips and he pulls me tighter against him until I can feel every hard line of his body.

"Have dinner with me tonight. I'll cook," I whisper against his lips, and he nods.

"Alright."

The timer starts to beep at me and I reluctantly pull away

from him and head back to the kitchen. By the time that I've pulled the croissants out of the oven, he's gone.

I change and get lost in work. Soon, customers start to pop in and I smile as I take orders and get started on prepping for tomorrow.

Ginger comes in as I'm about to flip the sign to closed, and I smile as she heads into the back to see what baked goods are left.

"How was today?" She asks as she hops up onto the counter.

"Good. Busy."

"Yeah? Any special guests?" She asks me with a wicked glint in her eyes.

"So, you know about Xavier then," I guess, and she grins.

"Yep. Maple called me this morning to tell me all about how he dropped you off and then came back for seconds."

I laugh at her wording, and she leans forward.

"So, your date went well then?"

"It did. I'm making him dinner tonight."

"Good. I'm happy for you, Olive."

"Thanks."

"Should I start looking for bridesmaid dresses?"

"No, we're not there yet. Not even close."

"I don't know. Maple said that with the way that he was looking at you this morning, she didn't think that wedding bells would be far off."

"Maple needs to have her eyes checked then," I tell her with a laugh. "He's just starting to let me in."

"I'll tell Maple to make an eye appointment then."

I laugh and finish wiping down the counters. Everything is ready for tomorrow, and I need to get going if I want to go home and take a shower before my date.

"I'll see you tomorrow," I tell Ginger, and she nods,

stuffing the last of her blueberry muffin into her mouth as she jumps off the counter.

We head up to the front door, and I grab the keys out of my pocket, searching for the bakery one. I hear Ginger snort, and she turns to me.

"Are you sure about those wedding bells?" She whispers, and I look past her to where Xavier is standing next to his truck, a bouquet of roses in his hands.

"Maybe not," I whisper.

She pats my arm as she heads over to the bookstore, and I smile as I take a step towards Xavier.

"For me?" I ask, and he smiles as he passes them to me.

"I had to run to the store and I saw them."

I smile. He might not be comfortable saying it outright, but it seems that Xavier thinks about me quite a bit.

"There I go, distracting you again," I sigh, and his eyes meet mine.

"Like I said, Olive. You've been distracting me since you got to town."

"With my pranks," I guess, and he frowns.

"No. With those eyes that are always so sparkly, like you know a joke and are just dying to let someone in on it. With that body. Fuck that body," he whispers, his eyes heating as they trail over me. "With this damn bakery and your fuck me pies."

"They're not called that," I interject, and he gives me a look.

"They practically are. Popping Cherries Pie? Fuck me," he groans, and I swallow hard.

"I'd love to."

His eyes darken even more with want, and I feel like I'm burning up. With one look this man can completely unravel me. He makes me want to try out every position that I've ever read about in my romance books.

"Let's go," he says softly, and I blink.

He offers me his hand, and I don't hesitate as I slide mine into it.

He leads me over to his truck and opens my door for me, his hands landing on my hips as he helps me into it.

"I was going to take you out to dinner," he says as he climbs behind the wheel, and I swallow as I turn to face him.

"I'm not hungry for food," I whisper, and he swallows.

"We're getting a pizza," he tells me, reversing out of the spot. "If we don't get food now, then I'll forget to feed you later."

"I can make us something," I argue, and he shakes his head.

"I'm taking care of you today. Even if it is only with pizza."

I smile to myself and he grabs my hand as we drive a street over to the Manci's Pizza Parlor.

"What toppings do you like?" He asks as we park.

"Pepperoni and mushrooms."

He nods and hops out of the truck.

"Sit tight. I'll be right back."

I nod, smiling as I watch him head inside. My phone buzzes, and I pull it out, smiling when I see Maple's name on the screen.

"Hey," I answer, and she squeals.

"Ginger told me about you and Xavier! Go girl!" She cheers, and I laugh.

"Thanks. We're grabbing pizza now and then heading home."

She sighs dreamily, like that's her dream date, and I grin. It might be. Maple has always been more of a homebody.

"Have fun. I'll be at the bakery first thing to hear all about it," she promises me, and I snort.

"That's not necessary."

"It is. I'll bring Saffron and Ginger with me."

"Great," I laugh, and I know that she's smiling too.

"See you then."

"Bye," I say, ending the call.

Xavier is already paying for the pizza, and a few minutes later, he's headed my way. He passes me the box, and I breathe in the scent of garlic and tomatoes.

He drives confidently towards our houses, and I study him. He's so handsome, so strong and capable. That mask that he used to wear has started to slip. In fact, right now, he looks happy and relaxed.

My heart soars at that, and I reach for his hand as he pulls onto our street.

"Your place or mine?" I ask, and he huffs out a laugh.

"How long have you wanted to ask someone that?" He asks, and I blush.

Part of me is surprised that he knows me so well. I'm not sure why. He's proven a few times now that he's been paying attention to me.

"A while," I admit, and he smiles as he turns to me.

"Which would you prefer?"

"Mine. I have to be at the bakery early tomorrow."

"Your place it is, then."

We climb out of his truck, and he carries the pizza as we head across the silent street to my little cottage. I unlock the door and let us in.

The air turns thick with tension as he stalks me into the kitchen. He tosses the pizza box onto the counter, and I swallow hard as he approaches me.

"Anything else that you've been dying to try?" He whispers against the shell of my ear.

"A few," I admit.

His lips find mine then, and I let him take over. He grabs my hips, lifting me onto the counter. A thrill runs through me every time that he manhandles me. Next to him, I feel small and dainty.

His fingers tilt my chin up so that he can devour me better, and I lean closer to him, wanting him to do just that.

My fingers go to his coat, and he unzips it impatiently, shrugging it off and letting it fall at his feet. I reach for the bottom of his Henley, and together we pull it over his head. He growls, not seeming to like that he had to stop kissing me and I hurry to tug off my coat and shirt.

His lips land on mine and I wrap my arms around his neck. His hands grip my ass and I gasp against his mouth as he lifts me.

"Bedroom?" He asks, and I point down the short hallway.

"Last door."

He nods, taking off in that direction, and I tighten my legs around his waist. I kiss a path up his neck and he shudders as I tug his earlobe between my teeth.

"You drive me crazy," he groans as we crash onto my bed.

"In a good way?" I ask, and he nods.

"In the best way."

He kisses the swell of my breasts and my fingers thread through his hair, holding him close. I feel his fingers on the snap of my jeans, and then his hand pushes into my panties, his fingers finding my clit and rubbing over that special spot.

"Oh!" I gasp, and I feel Xavier smile against my chest.

I push at my jeans, needing more of him, and he stands, dragging the pants and my panties down my legs and tossing them over his shoulder.

"You too," I tell him urgently, and he strips off the last of his clothes before he climbs back onto the bed.

"Need you," he grunts, and I nod.

"I need you too."

His lips find mine, and my hands slide over his back,

pulling him closer. I want to feel his weight on me. I want to feel every inch of him against me, in me.

"Need to get you ready," he says, and I smirk.

"Oh, I am. Trust me."

He smiles, kissing me once more before he shifts lower.

"Okay, then I need your taste on my tongue the first time that I fuck you. Spread your legs, baby. Real wide."

My core clenches at his dirty words, and I hurry to do as he orders.

"Good girl," he praises, and I nearly come from hearing him say those words.

"New kink unlocked," I mutter, and he glances up at me.

"What?" He asks, his thumbs spreading my pussy lips.

"I said new kink unlocked."

He frowns, and I try to pay attention to the conversation as his fingers play with me, driving me wild.

"I liked you calling me a good girl," I tell him breathlessly.

His eyes darken and heat and he gives me a wicked smile.

"Yeah?" He asks, and I nod frantically as one thick finger rubs over my opening.

He hooks just the tip of his finger inside of me and I whine, trying to clamp down around the digit.

"You want to be my good girl? To please me?" He asks.

"Oh god!" I gasp.

"You sucked my cock last night like a good girl. Swallowing me down so sweetly."

"Xavier…"

"Getting on your knees for me so quickly, wrapping those bee-stung lips around me without me even having to ask. Yeah… you can be my good girl," he says as his finger pushes in an inch.

I'm panting, already on the edge of an orgasm and he's barely touching me.

"Please!" I beg, and I can hear the smile in his voice when he responds.

"Good girl. Beg me to make you come."

"Xavier, please. I need you. Please, please, please make me come!"

I'm not sure when I started screaming. When Xavier's mouth lands on me, I realize that I don't care. We're the only two houses down here, so it's not like we're going to be disturbing anyone.

Xavier's tongue licks me and I shudder, twitching under him as he pins me in place. His finger sinks into me another inch and when his lips wrap around my clit, I come.

"Xavier!" I scream, my eyes closing as I have the most intense orgasm of my life.

"Good job, baby," he praises, and I blink my eyes open, my vision hazy as he climbs up my body.

I reach for him, and he grabs my hand, pinning it back to the mattress.

"I need you," he tells me, and I nod, spreading my legs wider.

The tip of his cock nudges against my dripping opening, and I look up into his dark eyes as he starts to push inside of me.

"Fuck. So damn tight," he says between gritted teeth.

"You're so big," I pant, and he nods, sweat starting to dot on his brow.

"You can take me."

I hook one leg around his waist, gasping as he sinks in another inch. My eyes flutter closed as he kisses me and then he's thrusting into me fully.

"Oh!" I gasp, my eyes flying open.

Xavier is peppering kisses all over my face, telling me how amazing I feel and how perfect I am.

I feel so full, but it's not necessarily a bad feeling. I clench around him, testing the new sensation, and Xavier curses, burying his face in my neck.

"Trying to make me come already," he groans, and I bite back a smile.

"I need you to move," I tell him, and he nods.

The first time his hips pull back and then push back in, I gasp. The second time, my hips rise to meet his. By the third time, I'm moaning and urging him to go harder and deeper.

"Olive, Olive, Olive," Xavier chants, his gaze locked with mine.

I can feel my core clenching around him, another orgasm starting to grow inside of me.

"I'm close," I tell him as he starts to pound into me.

"I know. I can feel this damn tight pussy trying to suck my come from me already. Such a greedy girl," he says, and I almost come from his words alone.

"Please, Xavier," I beg, and he reaches between us, his fingers finding my clit.

One stroke, two, and then I'm flying over the edge, screaming his name as I take him with me.

"Olive," he moans, and I wrap my arms around his neck, pulling him down for a kiss.

I can feel his release spreading inside of me, and I should probably be worried that we didn't use protection, but I can't find it in me to care right now. Not when I'm still riding my post-orgasm high.

"That was…" he starts, and I grin.

"Good?" I tease, and he smirks.

"Perfect."

"And it was our first time. Think that it can only get better?" I ask him, and he kisses my neck.

"Only one way to find out," he responds, and I moan as he starts to move in me once more.

CHAPTER 9

avier

"Explain to me why you woke me up and dragged me out here again?" Townes grumbles as we head into the mall.

"We need Christmas gifts."

"And you thought waiting until two days before Christmas was the best time to do this?" He asks, dodging a mom and dad who are wrangling two screaming kids.

"Yep. You need stuff too, remember? You're coming to their place too."

He nods, looking like he's headed into battle as he stares at the front doors of the mall. We head inside, stepping off to the side to look around.

"Alright. Where are we headed first?" Townes asks.

"I don't know. I wanted to get something for Olive."

"How about a ring?" He asks under his breath, but I hear him.

"And her sisters," I say, ignoring his comment.

"Okay… and what are you getting them?"

"I don't have a clue. I haven't bought anyone but you a gift in years."

"I'm honored."

"Shut up."

He sighs, and we turn to look around the crowded shops.

"Let's start there," I say, pointing to the first store.

We weave our way through the crowd and head inside. There's a bunch of soaps and spa items here and I grab a few things, hoping that the girls will like. Townes grabs some lotions and bath bombs, and we pay then head to the next store. We grab candles and hot chocolate gift sets at the next stores.

"This should be good, right?" Townes asks.

Both of us are loaded down with bags, but it doesn't feel like enough.

"Does this all seem kind of generic?" I ask him, and he sighs.

"I guess? But I think that they'll like it."

"I need to find Olive something else," I tell him, and he nods towards a jewelry store. "No… she needs new baking sheets."

"How romantic," Townes grumbles as we head towards the cookware store.

I ignore him. I know that Olive will love it. Her whole face lights up whenever I say or do something that she mentions. She's been taking care of everyone, paying attention to what they need so that she can give it to them, and I want to do the same for her. When I brought her those shoes yesterday, she looked at me like I was her hero. I want her to keep doing that.

We grab wrapping paper on our way to the checkout and then have to fight our way out of the mall and back to my truck. It's another forty minutes back to Wolf Valley, and I drop Townes off at his place first.

"See you tomorrow," I say as he hops out.

"See ya."

He grabs his bags and heads inside, and I smile as I drive back to my place. It's still early so I know that Olive is at the bakery. I debate heading that way, just so I can see her, but I should wrap the presents before she comes over tonight. I have a feeling that Olive is the type of person who would peek to see what you got her.

I smile at the thought as I park and start to carry everything inside. I'm unlocking the door when an old truck pulls into my driveway. My stomach sinks as soon as I see it.

"Dad," I say, dropping the bags inside the house and turning to meet him in the drive.

I don't want him to ever step foot inside of my house. I thought that we had agreed on that, albeit silently. I haven't seen him once since I moved back to town and it's been a blessing.

I take him in now. He still looks just as miserable as I remember, but his hair has more gray and his face is weathered. He looks a lot older than he is.

"What are you doing here?" I ask him.

"Nice to see you too, son," he says, that same bitter edge in his tone.

I want to say that it's not nice to see him. That I would be happier to never see him again, but I bite my tongue. I don't want to start a fight. I want him to say whatever it is that he came here for and then leave me the hell alone.

"I'm kind of busy," I start, and he looks around my property.

I can feel every muscle in my body tense just by being in his presence. All of those memories from my childhood slam into me and I feel on edge. I can hear his voice in my head, calling me worthless, promising that no one would ever love me and I start to grow dizzy.

I swallow, trying to blink away the black dots clouding my vision.

"I know. That's why I'm here," he says, and I blink.

"What?"

My dad's mouth flattens at that and I'm transported back to every time I was around my dad growing up. It didn't matter if I had gotten straight A's on my report card or when I enlisted. He has always been angry and disappointed in me.

Exhaustion swamps me and I lean against the railing on my porch.

"I've seen you around town with that little girl who runs the bakery."

I grit my teeth, waiting for him to go on, even though I already know what he's going to say.

"You need to leave her alone. Let her be happy. Let her be alive," he snarls at me, and I flinch.

"I didn't kill mom. It was an accident," I tell him, and he shakes his head.

"You would have been fine until the storm passed, but no, you just had to be selfish."

"I was sick," I stress.

I don't know why I bother. Nothing that I say will make any difference to him.

"I wish that it had been you," I whisper, and his angry blue eyes snap to mine.

"I wish that you had never been born. Everyone would be so much happier without you."

I stare at him, watching as he gives me a disgusted look and then turns to stomp off back to his truck.

I watch him leave before I head inside, feeling numb. I trip over the bags by the front door and suddenly I feel dumb for going through all of this trouble.

What did I think I was doing? Did I think that I could be with Olive? That my darkness wouldn't touch her? I should have stayed away from her. I should have kept her at arm's length, ignored her. I couldn't though. I let her in and now I'm going to have to push her away.

"So, turns out that I'm shit at wrapping presents," Townes says as he walks into my place.

I jump, startled. I didn't even hear him pull up.

I glance out the window and frown when I see that it's getting dark out. I must have gotten lost in old memories and stood there, frozen, for longer than I realized.

"What have you been doing?" Townes asks as he frowns down at the bags.

"My dad stopped by," I whisper, and his head snaps up to me.

I can see the mix of fury and sadness in his gaze. Townes is the only one who knows what seeing that man does to me. I may be twenty-six, but whenever I'm around him, I feel like I'm a little kid all over again.

"He told me to stay away from Olive."

"But you're not going to listen to him, right? Because he's a selfish drunk and doesn't know what he's talking about."

I can hear the venom in his voice, and I try to feel the same kind of anger. Anything would be better than this gnawing ache inside of me.

"Xavier," Townes sighs, and I swallow.

I glance across to Olive's house, and Townes groans.

"Don't, X. Don't sabotage this thing. It's good. You deserve good things."

I hear his words, but I just can't accept them. Not when I've been told the opposite my entire life.

"Let's go grab a beer," he suggests, but I shake my head.

"I just want to be alone right now."

He looks upset, but he nods and heads back towards the door.

"Just… don't do anything that you're going to regret. You don't need to push her away," he says.

I can't bring myself to even nod, and he sighs as he heads back outside.

I collapse onto the couch and stare at the empty fireplace as I debate what to do now.

CHAPTER 10

live

I HAD HOPED that Xavier would come in to see me yesterday or even today, but he didn't. When I had come by his place last night, he was gone and I must have been fast asleep by the time that he came back.

I try not to let his absence bother me, but I can't. My gut churns, and I know before I pull into my driveway and see him sitting on his front porch that something is wrong. Still, I try to pretend otherwise.

"Hey, you!" I say, pasting a smile on my lips as I climb out and head his way.

"Hey," he says, pushing to his feet.

I can see it then. Regret and resignation are written all over his face. For the first time since I've met him, I wish that his stoic mask was in place.

"Don't," I sigh and he blinks.

"What?"

"Don't do this."

I hate that I'm pleading with him. I know how awesome I am. I know that Xavier or any man would be damn lucky to have me.

"We were happy. What could have possibly happened?" I demand to know, and he shifts in the snow.

"I just can't do this. I'm not meant to be someone's boyfriend. I'm not meant for happily ever afters."

"You are. You're being dumb. What happened?" I ask again, and he looks away from me.

"I was reminded of who I am."

"By who?" I snap.

"My dad," he whispers and even though I feel for him, I'm just as pissed off and right now, the anger is winning.

"I didn't realize that your dad's opinion meant so much to you. Thought that you two weren't close."

"We aren't."

"Then why are you letting him get in the way of this?"

"It's not like that. He's right. I can't do this. I knew that I couldn't be with you or anyone else. It's why I avoided dating. It's why I avoided you for so long."

"Then why did you stop?" I yell, my hands balling up into fists.

"I couldn't… I couldn't stop."

He looks so heartbroken for a moment and I want to go to him and hug him, but then I remember that he's the one choosing to do this to us.

Suddenly, I'm so tired. All of the anger and hurt leave me and I'm left feeling numb and exhausted.

"Fine, Xavier. I'm not going to argue with you, but know this."

His eyes meet mine and he looks worried at what I'll say next.

"I was willing to chase you. I was willing to fight to make

you see just how great and loveable you really are. I can't keep fighting though. Not if you won't fight too."

He swallows hard, his dark gaze locked on me.

"You're going to wake up one day and realize that breaking up with me was a terrible mistake. You're going to regret it."

I turn then and head back to my place, and as I go, I can almost swear that I hear him murmur that he already does regret it.

It's probably just my imagination though, so I don't bother to turn around.

I head inside and bypass the kitchen, walking straight into my bedroom and collapsing onto my bed. Only then do I let my confident mask fall.

Tears spill onto my cheeks and I cry for everything that we lost and everything that we could have been.

avier

I'M busy shoveling my driveway when Townes pulls up and climbs out. He sighs when he sees me, and I grit my teeth, keeping my eyes on the driveway.

"Well, you look just as bad as Olive does this morning," he says, and I frown.

"Olive never looks bad," I grumble, and he scrubs his hands down his face.

"I'm guessing that you did what I told you not to and pushed her away last night instead of telling Olive that you're in love with her."

"We decided to stop seeing each other," I agree, and he swears under his breath.

"You're a moron."

My gaze snaps to his and I blink.

"What?" I ask, shoving my shovel into the snow bank so that it doesn't fall.

"You heard me. You're an idiot. You just dumped the girl that you're crazy about because what? You saw your dad?"

"It's not that," I grit out, and he rolls his eyes.

"It is. You're letting him get in your head and you shouldn't. That guy hasn't been a father or parent to you since you were a kid. He shouldn't have any control over you."

"I know that!" I shout.

He watches me, and I can feel myself splintering apart all over again. I thought that ending things with Olive last night was the worst pain, but rehashing it now, when the wound is still fresh, hurts just as bad.

"I know that, but I can't seem to turn it off."

"So, you're just going to be alone forever instead."

It feels like the air just got knocked out of me and I shift on my feet.

"What's the plan here, X? What are you going to do when Olive starts dating someone else? What are you going to do when she brings some other guy home?"

My hands tighten into fists and I see red at the thought.

"It's going to happen," he presses, and I snap.

I run my hands through my hair and start to pace.

"What happens if I hurt her?"

"X, think about it. Think about purposefully hurting Olive."

I recoil at the thought, feeling sick to my stomach, and he nods at me.

"You won't hurt her. You have this skewed idea of yourself where you seem to think that you're a bad guy, but you're not. You aren't responsible for your mom's death. It's not your fault that your dad is a prick."

I swallow and he keeps going.

"You're my best friend, man. I can't watch you destroy

yourself. Olive makes you happy. She's brought you out of that weird funk that you were in with all of her pranks."

I know that what he's saying is true. I was feeling bored, stuck in a rut, ever since I got out of the military. Even in the military, I'm not sure that I was happy.

"Maybe you should talk to someone. Come with me to the VA," Townes says, and I frown.

"You go to the VA?" I ask him, and he huffs out a laugh.

"Yeah, man. Turns out that I can't get shot at and almost blown up without bringing some of that shit home with me. I've been going to some group sessions for two months now."

I feel like a shit friend for not noticing that he was struggling and not knowing that he was going for so long.

"I didn't know that," I say quietly, and he nods.

"I know. You were getting settled back in town too and I didn't want to pile on. It's helped though. I think that it might help you too."

I nod, and he smiles slightly.

"Yeah, I'll try it."

"Good. Now, in the meantime, what are you going to do to fix this thing with Olive?"

I blow out a deep breath and look over to her empty house. She left bright and early this morning for the bakery. I know because I was awake and watched her leave through the front windows. I may have also snuck over there while she was sleeping to shovel her walkway and brush off her car, but she doesn't need to know that.

"I need to talk to her."

"Oh," Townes says, wincing, and I frown.

"What?" I ask him, and he shrugs.

"You're not great with words, man."

"Thanks," I deadpan, and he snorts.

"Women like big gestures, right? Maybe try that instead."

I pause, trying to come up with something to do to win Olive back. She said that she was willing to chase me and prove that I was worth being loved, but that she wanted to be chased too.

I guess I should take a note out of her playbook then.

"Alright… but I'm going to need your help."

Townes smiles at me as we head inside my place.

CHAPTER 12

live

I'M EXHAUSTED as I close up the bakery. My sisters have all stopped by at some point to check on me, but I'm afraid that I wasn't great company. They did their best to cheer me up and help out around the bakery, but after a bit, they had to get back to their own businesses.

The only good thing about today is that the bakery was slammed, so I didn't have any time to wallow in heartbreak. There were so many orders to be filled today and I'm glad that we're closed the next two days so that I can get a bit of a break.

I yawn as I head over to my car. I didn't get a ton of sleep last night after Xavier broke my heart. I'm looking forward to going home, taking a shower, and passing out. I'll need to be up early to get ready for my sisters to come over for Christmas tomorrow.

My heart breaks a little more as I wonder what Xavier will be doing tomorrow. Will he spend it all alone? With Townes?

I push thoughts of him out of my head as I climb behind the wheel and start to head home.

When I first see the lights, my first thought is that something is on fire. As I get closer though, I realize that it's Christmas lights that are spread out between Xavier's house and mine.

I pull to a stop in the middle of the road and step out, taking in the scene before me.

It takes me a minute to read what he's written in the lights.

I'm sorry. I'm an idiot. I love you.

"The idiot part was Townes' idea," Xavier says behind me, and I jump, spinning to face him.

"Well, he's right," I quip, and he smiles.

"I know."

We stare at each other, the lights casting yellow, green, and red shadows across our faces. There's so much that I want to say to him, so much I want to ask, but I'm done putting in all of the work here. Xavier messed up. He needs to be the one to fix it without any help or nudging from me. It's time for him to fight for me.

"Olive, I'm so sorry," he says, stepping towards me.

"For what?" I ask, taking a small step back.

He looks wounded at my movement but I don't let that sway me.

"For pushing you away. It was a mistake."

I'm silent, and he swallows hard, swaying towards me, but he stops himself before he takes another step.

"My dad came to see me yesterday."

"That's good, right? I mean, you said that you weren't close."

"We aren't. He stopped being my dad when my mom died. Seeing him is always such a mind fuck for me though," he admits and he looks so vulnerable.

"Seeing him just brought back everything that he said to me when my mom died. That it was my fault. That I was cursed and would hurt everyone that loved me."

"He's wrong."

"I know… or I'm trying to know that. I keep thinking that I'm okay and then something happens and I'm that scared kid again, who lost both his parents. I let him get to me yesterday and I should have just talked to you or Townes, but I didn't. I'm sorry for that. I'm sorry for hurting you, for breaking both of our hearts."

I swallow thickly, tears starting to well in my eyes.

"I talked to Townes this morning. He chewed me out and suggested that I talk to someone. I'm going to go to the VA with him once they are open again after the holidays. I'm going to work on myself, on being a man who is worthy of you."

"You've always been worthy of me," I choke out, and he smiles sadly.

"Then on being the best version of myself for you. So that I never hurt you again."

He takes a step towards me, and this time, I don't move away.

"What about that other thing?" I ask, pointing over my shoulder to where he's written that he loves me.

"I'm an idiot?" He asks, and I shake my head.

His eyes scan the lights, and I can see the moment that he realizes what I'm talking about.

"Oh… that."

He takes another step towards me, closing the distance between us, and I look up into his dark eyes.

"I love you, Olive. I have for a while, but I was too scared to admit it, even to myself. I'm done with being scared or holding myself back. I never stood a chance with you. I was always going to fall hopelessly in love with you."

The tears start to spill onto my cheeks now and Xavier looks devastated as he reaches to wipe them away.

"I'm sorry, please forgive me; I swear that I'll never hurt you again," he rambles as he brushes away more tears.

"Please, Olive," he begs. "I need you."

My throat is tight with tears, so instead of saying anything, I just lean up onto my tiptoes and press my lips to his.

He's frozen beneath me and I lean against him more, urging him to kiss me back. He moves then, his hands wrapping around my hips and pulling me into his chest more. His mouth moves against mine, licking along the seam of my lips until I open for him.

He tastes like cold, like snow, and I smile softly against his mouth.

"I'm sorry," he whispers against my lips and I shake my head.

"Just don't do it again," I warn him.

"Never," he swears.

Headlights bounce over us briefly, and I realize that we're still standing in the middle of the road, my car parked behind us, and the strings of lights creating a tangled mess all over both of our yards.

"We should clean this up," I say, and he nods.

"I can. You go inside and warm up."

"Well, if I help you clean up then you can help me warm up."

I give him a sultry look and he smiles.

"You're so smart."

I laugh and grab the first string of lights. I intended on

trying to untangle them and wrap them up, but when I look over at Xavier, he's just tugging the whole mess into his front yard.

"Well, that's one way to decorate," I comment, and he laughs.

The sound still comes out a little rusty, but I'm pleased that it seems to be coming easier.

He may still have a way to go before he's not such a grump, but I'm glad that I'll get to be by his side to help him.

Once the lights are all in his front yard, I move my car. I park in my driveway, and he opens the door for me. I smile up at him, and he leans down, claiming my lips in a steamy kiss that has me feeling warmer already.

"Let's get inside," I whisper. "Unless you want to take me up against the side of my house like that snowman couple over there."

He glances over to where his snowmen are still standing and smirks.

"I could, but I think that we'd both freeze before we finished."

"Speak for yourself," I say, and he laughs.

"You want to get fucked against a wall? That's fine, but I'm doing it inside, where I can really take my time after I make you come all over my cock."

I'm ready to combust and can only stare at him for a beat. He grins, bending and throwing me over his shoulder.

I giggle as he starts to head up to the front door. I pass him my keys and he unlocks the door and heads inside, kicking the door closed behind us.

"Any wall in particular?" He asks me, and I smile.

"Let's start with this one."

I point at the front door, and he slides me down his body as he turns and presses my back to the door.

"Start with? Ambitious."

"You love it," I tell him, and he grins.

"Yeah, I do. Now, are you ready to be my good girl?" He asks.

I nod, and then his lips are on mine and all I can do is feel as he makes love to me on every wall that I ask him to.

CHAPTER 13

avier

I NEVER REALLY THOUGHT THAT I was much of a holiday person. I barely celebrated them before, but now, being here in Olive's house, surrounded by people, I can start to see the appeal.

Olive is beaming, laughing at something that her sister, Saffron, says and I find myself smiling too. She's really in her element today, and for the first time in my life, I imagine what my future will be like with her in it. I'm sure that it will be filled with laughter and love. With family.

The little ball of fur in my lap stretches and I look down at my new puppy. I had been shocked when Olive had gone out to meet her sisters and walked through the door with the black and white pup and even more surprised when she promptly handed him off to me.

"Merry Christmas!"

"A dog?" I asked, and she laughed.

"Every grinch needs a trusty companion."

She and her sisters had giggled at that, but I was touched. The little guy licked my nose and I fell in love with him then and there. I decided to name him Max in honor of How the Grinch Stole Christmas, and everyone agreed that was the perfect name for him.

Max spent the morning tearing apart wrapping paper and fighting with ribbons. I thought that I had all of the family that I needed with Townes, but Olive has shown me how wrong I was about that. It's not a bad thing to have people that you care about. It's a good thing. It just might take some time for me to get used to having so many people around, but I'm looking forward to it.

I glance over at Townes and see him looking a little bewildered. That's exactly how I felt when everyone started to arrive. It's been a lifetime since either of us has had this and I'm glad that Olive invited both of us.

"Sorry," Mira says as she stumbles into me.

I reach out to steady her, and she smiles gratefully.

"Word of warning, Maple appears to have spiked the eggnog already," she whispers to me, and I grin.

"Then I don't think that you'll be needing anymore of this," Townes says as he plucks the cup from her fingers.

"Hey!" Mira protests, and I stare at Townes in shock.

I didn't even see him headed over here. I've also never heard him talk to anyone like that. Normally, he avoids everyone just like me.

"I'll just get another," she tells him.

This is the most that I've ever heard her talk, and I wonder just how much liquid courage she's had already today to be standing up to Townes right now.

"No, you won't."

They glare at each other for a beat and I clear my throat, giving Townes a what the fuck look. He ignores me and goes back to watching Mira with narrowed eyes as she heads back towards the kitchen.

"Dude, are you feeling okay?" I ask him as he downs the eggnog.

"Yeah, why?"

"Well, for one, you're bossing around girls that you barely know, and two, you fucking hate eggnog."

He glowers at me, and I blink when I see what's going on here.

"Ah," I say, lifting my cup of hot chocolate to my lips to hide my smile.

I still can barely stomach the stuff, but it's starting to grow on me. It reminds me of Olive and what she tasted like the other night. I push those thoughts from my head before I embarrass myself by getting a hard-on right here at Christmas dinner.

"Don't *ah* me," Townes snaps, and I cough, trying to cover up my laugh.

"When do you think the wedding will be?" I tease him, and he curses under his breath and heads off after Mira.

"Hey, you. Are you having fun?" Olive asks as she comes over to my side.

"Yeah, I am. Townes is, too."

She nods, watching as my best friend stares across the kitchen at Mira. He's watching her like a hawk, and she's doing her best to pretend like he doesn't exist. It would probably be a lot easier if Townes wasn't six and a half feet tall.

"Good," Olive says with a knowing smile.

"What can I help with?" I ask her for the hundredth time today.

I tried to help her in the kitchen this morning, but we ended up burning the cinnamon rolls instead. I should have known something like that would happen. We can't seem to be in the same room as each other without wanting to rip each other's clothes off.

I was banished from the kitchen after that and spent the morning cleaning and rearranging furniture so everyone would fit. I promised to handle clean up so that Olive could get a break, and that had earned me a very special thank you, one that I was all too happy to return.

I brought over all of my presents while she redid the cinnamon rolls, and by then, everyone was starting to arrive.

Olive's sisters and Mira all loved their gifts. They had gotten Townes and I flannel shirts, and we had all laughed when they realized that they all got us the same thing. I gave Olive her baking sheets and she had teared up a bit, which earned her a teasing from her sisters, but she ignored them. I had smirked at Townes and he just rolled his eyes in return.

"Nothing. Dinner is all set. I just need to carry it over to the table," Olive tells me.

"Townes and I will do that."

She smiles up at me and my heart flips over in my chest. I lean down, pressing my lips to hers and I feel her smile widen against my mouth.

"I love you, Olive."

"Good, because I love you too."

I stand and head over to the kitchen, bringing the first dish to where we slid some tables together in the living room. Townes is right behind me, and in no time, we've got the food brought over, and everyone is taking a seat.

I pull out Olive's chair and she grins up at me in thanks.

I'm so in love with her. I know that if she hadn't moved to my town and started to screw with me, I would still be that sad shell walking around town. She came here and woke me up. She made me see what I was missing.

I can't wait to see what the future has in store for both of us.

"Dig in!" Olive announces and I smile as we all do as she commands.

I'm going to marry this girl.

That thought would have scared me, but with Olive, it feels right. I know that I need to work on myself; to be the best version I can be for her, but then, I'm going to put a ring on her finger and make her mine.

I imagine next Christmas with Olive by my side, a ring on her finger and her belly swollen with our baby.

Suddenly, I can't wait for the future.

CHAPTER 14

live

FIVE YEARS LATER...

"IN A FEW YEARS, you're not going to be able to leave Elfie here in these kinds of positions," Xavier warns me as he comes into our bedroom to see me rearranging our Elves on a Shelf.

"These two are just for us," I promise him, and he grins as he comes over and wraps his arms around my waist.

"Are we doing that position tonight?" He whispers in my ear, and I smirk at him over my shoulder.

"Think you're up for it?" I ask him and he growls in response, grinding his erection against my ass.

"I'm always up for you."

He kisses his way down my neck and I smile, leaning back against him.

"The kids are coming," I tell him as I hear their little feet headed to our room.

He sighs, giving me one last kiss as he turns to greet them.

"Dad!" Our twins say in unison, and I smile as Xavier drops to his knees to pick them up.

The girls' hair is still wet from their bath, and I laugh when I see that Brie's pajamas are on backwards.

"Ready for a bedtime story?" Xavier asks them, and they cheer, giggling as they take off back toward their room.

Xavier and I got married four Christmases ago and he moved me into his house right after. I kept my cottage and we've been renting it out online. Xavier handles all of the upkeep and bookings and I know that he's happy to be able to handle that for me.

I still run the bakery, though I've hired more people since we had the girls. Brie and Hazel were born almost ten months to the date of our wedding. It had been such a shock for both of us when we were told that we were having twins, but Xavier stepped up. He supported me and did so much when I was pregnant and he's been the best dad to both of them since the moment that they were born.

I know that he was worried when he found out that I was pregnant and he actually went back to see his therapist at the VA to talk over some things. I'm so proud of him and how hard he's worked to let go of the hurtful things that his dad said to him in the past.

A knock sounds at the door and Xavier frowns. Max heads down the hall to check it out.

"Are we expecting anyone?" He asks me, and I shake my head.

"No, you go see who it is, and I'll get the girls tucked in and ready for their story."

He nods, heading downstairs, and I smile as I head into

the girls' room. Having twins is quite the handful, and Xavier and I both decided that we were done after the girls turned one. The pregnancy had been hard on me, and the birth had been rough on Xavier. I had to have an emergency c-section, and I think almost losing all of us really scared him.

"What are we reading tonight?" I ask Hazel and Brie as I pull the covers over them.

"Goodnight, Moon!" Brie says, and I smile.

It's her favorite book so I'm not surprised.

"I want a Christmas book!" Hazel announces and I laugh as I head over to their bookshelf and grab How The Grinch Stole Christmas.

"Do we have any honey or lemon?" Xavier asks, and I frown.

"For what?"

"It's Townes here. Mira's not feeling well. Says her throat hurts, but the market is closed."

My phone buzzes, and I pull it out.

MIRA: I'm so sorry! I told Townes to just wait until the morning. It's just the sniffles.

Olive: No worries! You know how these men are.

I SEND her a laughing emoji and hand the books to Xavier.

"I'll grab the honey and lemon juice for Townes. You get started on bedtime."

He smiles, glancing down at the books and I hear him laugh at Hazel's choice as I head into the kitchen.

"Hey, Townes. How's it going?"

"Good. Sorry to interrupt so late."

"No worries. I hope that Mira feels better soon," I say as I pass him the bottles.

"She will," he says like he alone has control over that.

Xavier and him are so alike. Both would do anything for their families; both are still fighters.

I smile and walk him to the door.

"See you tomorrow. Let us know if you need anything else."

"Will do. Have a good night."

He heads over to his truck, and I close and lock the front door before I head back to the girls' room.

Xavier is halfway through Goodnight, Moon, so I sneak down the hall and into our room. I'm putting on his early Christmas present when the door opens and Xavier grounds to a halt.

His eyes widen and darken as he takes me in, and I pout.

"You ruined the surprise."

"Oh, I'm surprised," he assures me, and I smile, spinning around so that he can see me from all angles.

"There were high heels and stockings too," I say as I walk towards him.

"You don't need them," he promises me.

He's already reaching for me before I'm even close enough for him to grab me and I grin.

"Merry Christmas Eve," I whisper against his lips and he grins.

"Now I feel bad," he murmurs, and I look up at him.

"Why?"

"Cause I didn't get you anything," he says with a devilish smirk.

I laugh, wrapping my arms around his neck.

"Oh, don't worry. I'm sure you can think of something to give me."

He laughs as he tightens his arms around me and carries me over to the bed.

Where he proceeds to give me two very good gifts.

* * *

Looking for more Wolf Valley holiday books? Check out Townes and the Baker sisters books here, starting with A Very Grumpy Valentine's Day!

Don't miss the other Grumpy books! Check out A Very Grumpy Best Friend and the other Wolf Valley Grumps here!

ABOUT THE AUTHOR

CONNECT WITH ME!

If you enjoyed this story, please consider leaving a review on Amazon or any other reader site or blog that you like. Don't forget to recommend it to your other reader friends.

If you want to chat with me, please consider joining my VIP list or connecting with me on one of my Social Media platforms. I love talking with each of my readers. Links below!

Website
Newsletter

<u>Folklore</u>

<u>Kidnapping His Forever</u>

<u>Claiming His Forever</u>

<u>Finding His Forever</u>

<u>Rescuing His Forever</u>

<u>Chasing His Forever</u>

<u>Folklore: The Complete Series</u>

<u>Holiday Hearts</u>

Be Mine

Falling in Love

Holly Jolly Holidays

<u>Love Notes</u>

<u>Signing Off With Love</u>

<u>Care Package Love</u>

<u>Wrong Number, Right Love</u>

<u>Kings Gym</u>

Fighting Fire With Fire

Fighting Tooth and Nail

Fighting Back From Hell

<u>Mine To</u>

<u>Mine to Love</u>

<u>Mine to Protect</u>

<u>Mine to Cherish</u>

<u>Mine to Keep</u>

Mine to: The Complete Series

<u>Sequoia: Stud Farm</u>

Branded

Bucked

Roped

Spurred

<u>**Sequoia: Fast Love Racing**</u>

Jump Start

Pit Stop

Home Stretch

<u>Telltale Heart</u>

<u>Bought and Paid For</u>

<u>His Miracle</u>

<u>Pretty Girl</u>

<u>Telltale Hearts Boxset</u>